MW01104194

elegant
endings

Published by:
TRIDENT REFERENCE PUBLISHING
801 12th Avenue South, Suite 400
Naples, Fl 34102 USA

Tel: + 1 (239) 649-7077
www.tridentreference.com
email: sales@tridentreference.com

Elegant Endings
© TRIDENT REFERENCE PUBLISHING

Publisher
Simon St. John Bailey

Editor-in-chief
Susan Knightley

Prepress
Precision Prep & Press

Includes Index
ISBN 1582797285
UPC 6 15269 97285 4

Printed in The United States

introduction

The world consists of only two kinds of people
–those who merely enjoy dessert and those who
would die for a taste of sweet heaven.
If you're one of the latter, this is the book for you.
Fruit and nuts delights, chocolaty temptations,
custards and parfaits, mousses and ice creams,
crêpes and puddings, pies, rolls and cakes –they
are all here in abundance.

elegant endings
introduction

For a special occasion, a fabulous home-cooked dinner followed by a spectacular dessert is the perfect way to celebrate. So we have focused on stylish ideas for entertaining, but there are also a few childhood favorites with their timeless goodness.

Some of the desserts in this book are quick and easy, while others take a little more time to prepare, but are well worth the effort. You can be sure that every recipe has been thoroughly tested by our cookery team. They really do work and they taste as marvelous as they look.

Quick Decorating Ideas

- Flaked almonds, chopped nuts (such as pistachios, pecans and macadamias), grated chocolate are all good for sprinkling creamy desserts or decorating the sides of cakes.
- Fruit coulis or warmed sieved jam can add extra flavor and color to cheesecakes, pies and crêpes.

- Some shredded coconut, sifted cocoa powder or ground cinnamon will be great for warm puddings.
- Glacé and dried fruits or crushed meringue will look wonderful on the top of cakes and gâteaux.
- Wafer biscuit rolls are a must to accompany ice creams, mousses and parfaits.
- Frosted rose petals and violets give chocolate desserts a touch of class.
- Strawberries half dipped in melted chocolate are almost a dessert on their own and can be used as decoration as well.
- Sifted icing sugar and fresh mint leaves are the simplest decorations of all –they go well with everything... and they never fail!

How to Frost Petals

Rinse petals and drain well on absorbent kitchen paper.

Place an egg white in a small bowl and whisk lightly. Dip petals in egg white. Remove, set aside to drain slightly, then coat with caster sugar.

Stand on a wire rack to dry for 2 hours or until set.

Difficulty scale

■□□I Easy to do

■■□I Requires attention

■■■I Requires experience

fruits
with cognac mascarpone

■□□ | Cooking time: 10 minutes - Preparation time: 10 minutes

method

1. Combine blueberries, strawberries, peaches and raspberries in a bowl. Place fruit in a shallow ovenproof dish and sprinkle with brown sugar. Cook under a hot grill for 8 minutes or until sugar melts and caramelizes.

2. To serve, place a mound of mascarpone on each serving plate, make a well in the center, sprinkle with caster sugar and fill well with cognac. Surround with hot fruit and serve immediately.

ingredients

> **250 g/8 oz blueberries**
> **250 g/8 oz strawberries, hulled and halved**
> **4 peaches, peeled and quartered**
> **250 g/8 oz raspberries**
> **125 g/4 oz brown sugar**
> **750 g/1¹/₂ lb mascarpone**
> **2 tablespoons caster sugar**
> **60 ml/2 fl oz cognac**

....
Serves 4

tip from the chef

Any fresh fruits can be served this attractive way.

pears
with macaroon filling

■□□ | Cooking time: 35 minutes - Preparation time: 10 minutes

ingredients

> **6 canned pear halves, drained**
> **3/4 cup crushed macaroons**
> **1 egg yolk, beaten**
> **2 tablespoons superfine sugar**
> **3 tablespoons butter, softened**

method

1. Scoop a little of the flesh from pear halves to make a deeper cavity. Add chopped flesh to crushed macaroons in a heatproof bowl. Stir in egg yolk, sugar and butter. Stir over a saucepan of simmering water until blended. Cool.

2. Spoon mixture into pear halves. Arrange in a greased ovenproof dish and bake at 180°C/350°F/Gas 4 for 25-30 minutes, or until golden. Serve with cream or ice cream, if desired.

....
Serves 6

tip from the chef
You can make this recipe with canned peach halves if you prefer.

figs with rum sauce

■ ■ □ | Cooking time: 20 minutes - Preparation time: 20 minutes

method

1. To make toffee, place sugar and water in a saucepan, stir over a low heat until sugar dissolves, brushing down crystals from sides of pan with a brush dipped in hot water. Bring to the boil and boil rapidly until toffee turns a golden brown. Remove from heat and stand saucepan in cold water. Allow bubbles to subside and pour toffee onto an oiled, upside-down baking tray. Set aside to set.

2. To make sauce, just prior to serving, place egg yolks, sugar and rum in a heatproof bowl over a saucepan of simmering water. Cook, beating continuously with an electric mixer, until sugar dissolves and mixture is creamy. Whisk in cream and continue to cook until sauce is heated through.

3. To serve, break toffee into splinters. Spoon sauce into dessert plates and place figs in the center. Decorate with toffee.

ingredients

> 4 fresh figs, cut into quarters

toffee

> 375 g/12 oz sugar
> 375 ml/12 fl oz water

sauce

> 6 egg yolks
> 185 g/6 oz caster sugar
> 3 tablespoons rum
> 315 ml/10 fl oz cream

....
Serves 4

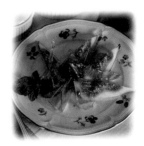

tip from the chef

Luscious figs served on a creamy sauce are sure to tickle the taste buds even after the hottest meal.

toffee *oranges*

■■□ I Cooking time: 10 minutes - Preparation time: 20 minutes

ingredients

> **6 oranges**
> **90 g/3 oz sugar**
> **60 ml/2 fl oz Grand Marnier**
> **4 whole cloves**
> **1 cinnamon stick**

toffee

> **500 g/1 lb sugar**
> **170 ml/5^1/$_2$ fl oz water**

method

1. Cut 10 long thin strips of peel from oranges, using a sharp knife or vegetable peeler. Cut peel into smaller strips and blanch in boiling water. Drain and reserve liquid.
2. Remove remaining peel and pith from oranges and discard. Place oranges in a bowl with sugar, Grand Marnier, 60 ml/2 fl oz reserved blanching liquid, cloves and cinnamon stick. Cover and refrigerate overnight.
3. To make toffee, place sugar and water in a saucepan. Cook over a medium heat, stirring constantly until sugar dissolves. Bring to the boil. Continue to cook, without stirring, until light golden.
4. Arrange oranges on a serving platter, sprinkle with strips of peel and spin toffee over.

....
Serves 6

tip from the chef

This light, simple and stunning dessert is ideal to serve after a substantial meal.
To spin toffee, coat the back of two wooden spoons with toffee, place them back to back and gently pull apart. As a thread of toffee is formed continue bringing spoons together and pulling apart until toffee starts to set. Repeat to use all the toffee.

snowballs

■□□ | Cooking time: 15 minutes - Preparation time: 20 minutes

method

1. Stand pears in a large saucepan with water to a depth of 1 cm/1/2 in. Cover and simmer for 8-10 minutes, or until just tender. Cool.
2. Beat egg whites until soft peaks form. Add sugar, a spoonful at a time, beating well after each addition. Continue to beat until meringue is thick and glossy.
3. Cover pears with meringue. Chop coconut roughly and sprinkle over pears. Top with almonds.
4. Place on a greased baking tray. Bake at 180°C/350°F/Gas 4 for 5 minutes, or until meringue is lightly browned.

ingredients

> 4 ripe pears, peeled, stems left intact
> 2 egg whites
> 5 tablespoons superfine sugar
> 1 cup shredded coconut
> 1 1/2 tablespoons sliced almonds

Serves 4

tip from the chef

If pears are not in season, you can use apples or canned pears instead. In summer do not miss trying fresh peaches prepared this way.

dates
with orange filling

■■□ | Cooking time: 0 minute - Preparation time: 20 minutes

method

1. Remove stones from dates, by cutting through center of dates lengthways then opening them out. Place cognac, cinnamon and cardamom in a glass dish and mix to combine. Add dates and toss well to coat. Cover and set aside to macerate for 1 hour.

2. To make filling, place mascarpone, icing sugar, orange rind and juice in a mixing bowl and beat until light and fluffy. Spoon mascarpone mixture into a piping bag fitted with a medium-sized fluted nozzle.

3. Remove dates from cognac mixture using a slotted spoon. Pat dry with absorbent kitchen paper, then pipe mascarpone mixture into the center of each date. Refrigerate until required. Serve with halved orange slices and rind strips.

....
Serves 4

ingredients

> **315 g/10 oz fresh dates**
> **¼ cup/60 ml/2 fl oz cognac**
> **¼ teaspoon ground cinnamon**
> **¼ teaspoon ground cardamom**
> **1 orange, peeled and sliced**
> **fine strips orange rind**

orange filling

> **125 g/4 oz mascarpone**
> **4 teaspoons icing sugar**
> **2 teaspoons finely grated orange rind**
> **4 teaspoons orange juice**

tip from the chef

These dates may be served as an after-dinner treat accompanied by a cup of rich coffee.

berry peach parfaits

■□□ | Cooking time: 0 minute - Preparation time: 20 minutes

ingredients

> 200 g/6$^1/2$ oz ricotta cheese
> 1 cup/200 g/6$^1/2$ oz natural yogurt
> $^1/4$ cup/60 ml/2 fl oz maple syrup
> 1 tablespoon orange-flavored liqueur
> 500 g/1 lb mixed berries of your choice, such as blueberries and raspberries or strawberries and blackberries
> 440 g/14 oz canned peach slices, drained
> 6 strawberries, halved
> $^1/2$ cup/45 g/1$^1/2$ oz shredded coconut, toasted

method

1. Place ricotta cheese, yogurt, maple syrup and liqueur in a bowl and beat until smooth.
2. Place a layer of ricotta mixture into the base of a parfait glass, top with a layer of mixed berries, then a second layer of ricotta mixture, a layer of peaches and a final layer of ricotta mixture. Decorate with strawberries and coconut. Repeat with remaining fruit and ricotta mixture to make 6 desserts.

....
Serves 6

tip from the chef

For a dessert lower in fat use low fat ricotta cheese and low fat yogurt.

nut
bavarian cream

a   b   c

■ ■ □ | Cooking time: 20 minutes - Preparation time: 15 minutes

method

1. To make praline, place water and sugar in a small saucepan and stir over a medium heat until sugar dissolves. Brush down sides of pan with a wet pastry brush. Bring to the boil and cook for 5-7 minutes or until toffee turns golden brown. Add hazelnuts and pour over a greased, upside-down baking tray (a). When cool, break into pieces and crush in a food processor or blender.

2. To make custard, combine egg yolks and sugar in a heatproof bowl. Place over a saucepan of simmering water and beat until a ribbon trail forms. Gradually add milk (b) and vanilla essence, stirring constantly. Transfer to a heavy-based saucepan and cook over a low heat, stirring in a figure-eight pattern, until custard thickens and coats the back of a wooden spoon. Do not allow to boil. Remove pan from heat and place in a bowl of ice. Stir until custard cools a little. Strain through a fine sieve if necessary.

3. Stir gelatin mixture into custard. Place over ice to cool, stirring occasionally. Fold whipped cream (c) and praline into custard as it begins to set. Spoon mixture into chocolate cases and refrigerate until set.

Serves 10

ingredients

> 1 tablespoon gelatin dissolved in 3 tablespoons boiling water and cooled
> 1 cup/250 ml/8 fl oz cream, whipped
> 10 chocolate cases

praline

> 4 tablespoons water
> 1 cup/250 g/8 oz sugar
> 125 g/4 oz hazelnuts, toasted

custard

> 3 egg yolks
> 1 1/2 tablespoons sugar
> 300 ml/10 fl oz milk, scalded
> 1/2 teaspoon vanilla essence

tip from the chef

These creamy surprises are laced with a hazelnut praline, a delight to end any special meal. In this recipe the cream is served in chocolate cases, but if you wish you can place it in individual molds.

wild
blueberry brûlée

■□□ I Cooking time: 20 minutes - Preparation time: 10 minutes

ingredients
> 2 x 450 g/14¹/2 oz cans wild blueberries, drained
> 6 egg yolks
> ³/4 cup sugar
> 2¹/2 cups thickened cream
> 1¹/2 tablespoons cold butter, cut into tiny cubes
> 2 tablespoons sugar, extra

method
1. Divide blueberries between 4 heatproof dishes and set aside.
2. Whisk egg yolks and sugar in a heatproof bowl over a saucepan of simmering water until thick and fluffy, about 7 minutes.
3. Pour cream into the egg mixture, whisking constantly until custard coats the back of a spoon, about 10 minutes. Remove from heat and whisk in butter. Pour custard over blueberries and chill for 10 minutes.
4. Just before serving, sprinkle extra sugar over the top and place dishes under a moderate grill to caramelize, about 1 minute.

....
Serves 4

tip from the chef
It is important to caramelize sugar at the last moment to avoid hardening. Serve with ice cream, if desired.

lime
and coconut custard

■□□ | Cooking time: 70 minutes - Preparation time: 15 minutes

method

1. Beat eggs, egg yolks and sugar in a bowl until light and fluffy.
2. Combine coconut milk, cream and milk in a saucepan and heat until almost boiling. Remove from heat and set aside to cool slightly.
3. Gradually pour milk mixture into egg mixture and beat until combined. Mix in coconut and lime rind.
4. Pour custard into a buttered 600 ml/1 pt capacity ovenproof dish. Stand dish in a baking pan and add enough boiling water to come halfway up the sides of the dish. Bake at 180°C/350°F/Gas 4 for 1 hour or until set.
5. Remove from oven and spoon into serving glasses. Dust with nutmeg and decorate with shredded coconut and lime rind. Serve warm.

ingredients

> **3 eggs**
> **4 egg yolks**
> **185 g/6 oz caster sugar**
> **375 ml/12 fl oz coconut milk**
> **125 ml/4 fl oz cream**
> **250 ml/8 fl oz milk**
> **375 g/12 oz desiccated coconut**
> **2 tablespoons grated lime rind**
> **ground nutmeg**
> **toasted shredded coconut**
> **lime rind**

....
Serves 6

tip from the chef

For an interesting temperature contrast, accompany this wintry dessert with chilled whipped cream.

frozen
zabaglione

■ ■ □ | Cooking time: 5 minutes - Preparation time: 25 minutes

method

1. Place egg yolks and sugar in a heatproof bowl and beat until mixture is pale and thick and forms a ribbon.
2. Combine rum, cognac and marsala and gradually whisk into egg yolk mixture. Place bowl over simmering water and whisk until mixture becomes soft and foamy. Remove from heat and set aside to cool. Fold cream into egg mixture.
3. Beat egg whites until soft peaks form, gradually add icing sugar and continue beating until combined. Fold 2 tablespoons egg whites mixture into egg yolk mixture, then gently fold into remaining egg whites mixture.
4. Place one-third mixture in a bowl and stir in coffee. Fold chocolate into remaining mixture.
5. Spoon half chocolate mixture into a 10 x 25 cm/4 x 10 in loaf tin lined with foil, smooth top with a spatula and freeze until firm. Spoon coffee mixture over, level with a spatula and return to freezer until firm. Spread remaining chocolate mixture over, level with a spatula and return to freezer. Freeze overnight.

ingredients

> 5 egg yolks
> 125 g/4 oz caster sugar
> 2 tablespoons rum
> 2 tablespoons cognac
> 4 tablespoons dry marsala
> 250 ml/8 fl oz double cream, lightly whipped
> 4 egg whites
> 125 g/4 oz icing sugar
> 2 teaspoons instant coffee dissolved in 1 tablespoon water
> 60 g/2 oz dark chocolate, grated

....
Serves 6

tip from the chef

This rich version of zabaglione is flavored with rum, cognac, coffee and chocolate in addition to the classic marsala.

rocky road
ice cream

■□□ | Cooking time: 0 minute - Preparation time: 10 minutes

method

1. Place ice cream in a large mixing bowl, fold in Turkish delight, peanut bars, pink and white marshmallows, red and green cherries and coconut.
2. Spoon mixture into a freezerproof container, cover and freeze until firm.
3. To serve, place scoops of ice cream into bowls.

....
Serves 6

ingredients

> 1 liter/1³/4 pt vanilla ice cream, softened
> 2 x 60 g/2 oz chocolate-coated Turkish delight bars, chopped
> 2 x 45 g/1¹/2 oz chocolate-coated scorched peanut bars, chopped
> 10 pink marshmallows, chopped
> 5 white marshmallows, chopped
> 6 red glacé cherries, chopped
> 6 green glacé cherries, chopped
> 4 tablespoons shredded coconut, toasted

tip from the chef

Serving suggestion: accompany with wafers. This ice cream is ideal for kids and will delight adults as well.

passion
fruit mousse

■□□ | Cooking time: 15 minutes - Preparation time: 15 minutes

ingredients

> 200 g/6½ oz low fat
  ricotta cheese
> 125 ml/4 fl oz reduced
  fat cream
> 2 tablespoons icing sugar
> 1 tablespoon gelatin
  dissolved in
  2 tablespoons hot water
> 60 ml/2 fl oz passion fruit
  pulp
> 3 egg whites

orange sauce

> 200 ml/6½ fl oz fresh
  orange juice, strained
> 100 ml/3½ fl oz apple
  juice
> 2 tablespoons sugar
> 2 teaspoons cornflour
  blended with 2 tablespoons
  water

method

1. Place ricotta cheese, cream and icing sugar
   in a food processor or blender and process
   until smooth. Stir in gelatin mixture
   and passion fruit pulp. Mix well.
2. Beat egg whites until soft peaks form, fold
   into passion fruit mixture. Spoon mixture
   into 6 individual 125 ml/4 fl oz capacity
   rinsed molds. Refrigerate until set.
3. To make sauce, combine orange juice,
   apple juice and sugar in a saucepan
   and cook over a low heat, stirring frequently,
   until sugar dissolves. Bring to the boil, then
   reduce heat and simmer for 3 minutes. Stir
   in cornflour mixture and cook over
   a medium heat, stirring frequently, until
   sauce boils and thickens. Remove from
   heat and set aside to cool. Refrigerate until
   well chilled. Turn out mousses and serve
   with sauce.

....
Serves 6

tip from the chef
*Low fat ricotta cheese and reduced fat cream
make this a "not-so-wicked" dessert for the
health conscious. Orange sauce is a perfect
alternative to cream.*

orange
pecan mousse

■□□ I Cooking time: 15 minutes - Preparation time: 20 minutes

method

1. To make praline, melt sugar in a small, heavy saucepan over low heat, stirring once or twice, then cook until golden brown. Add pecans, pour onto an oiled upside-down baking tray, cool. Break into pieces, saving a few pecan halves for decoration. Crush remainder in a food processor.

2. Beat egg whites until soft peaks form and gradually beat in sugar. Fold in cream, crushed praline and caramelized peel. Pour mixture into a large deep ring tin, cover with foil and refrigerate overnight.

3. To make sauce, scald milk with orange rind, remove from heat. Beat egg yolks with sugar until pale and thick. Gradually stir in hot milk, then return mixture to saucepan. Cook over low heat, stirring, until custard coats the spoon. Strain and set aside.

4. Turn mousse onto a serving platter and decorate with reserved pecan pieces and extra caramelized peel. Accompany with sauce.

ingredients

> 6 egg whites
> 140 g/4½ oz sugar
> 600 ml/1 pt double cream, whipped
> 1 tablespoon finely chopped caramelized peel
> caramelized peel, extra, to decorate

praline
> 125 g/4 oz sugar
> 60 g/2 oz pecan halves

custard sauce
> 600 ml/1 pt milk
> rind of 1 orange
> 6 egg yolks
> 90 g/3 oz sugar

Serves 12

tip from the chef

To caramelize peel, remove rind from 2 oranges, scrape off pith and cut peel into matchsticks. Place in a small saucepan, cover with cold water, bring to the boil, drain and refresh under cold water. Return peel to pan, add 60 g/2 oz sugar and enough water to moisten. Cook over moderate heat until sugar dissolves and liquid evaporates. Remove from heat and set aside to cool.

chilled
peach cream

■□□ | Cooking time: 0 minute - Preparation time: 15 minutes

method

1. Drain peaches, reserving syrup. Purée peaches in a blender or food processor. Measure purée to make 1¹/4 cups. Reserve remaining purée.
2. Sprinkle gelatin over 4 tablespoons reserved syrup, dissolve over a saucepan of simmering water, cool.
3. Whisk gelatin mixture into peach purée (a). Fold in cream (b).
4. Pour mixture into a rinsed fluted mold or 6 individual molds (c). Chill until set. Turn out and serve with remaining purée. Accompany with cream and fresh fruit if desired.

....
Serves 6

ingredients

> **840 g/28 oz canned peaches in syrup**
> **3 teaspoons gelatin**
> **1 cup double cream, whipped**

tip from the chef

To dissolve gelatin in the microwave, cook on High (100%) for 40 seconds.

a

b

c

crêpes suzette

■□□ | Cooking time: 20 minutes - Preparation time: 15 minutes

method

1. To make crêpes, place flour, milk, water, eggs, butter and sugar in a food processor or blender and process until smooth. Cover and set aside to stand for 1 hour.

2. Pour 2-3 tablespoons batter into a heated, lightly greased 18 cm/7 in crêpe pan and tilt pan so batter covers base thinly and evenly. Cook over a high heat for 1 minute or until lightly browned. Turn crêpe and cook on second side for 30 seconds. Remove from pan, set aside and keep warm. Repeat with remaining batter to make 12 crêpes.

3. Fold crêpes into quarters and arrange overlapping in a heatproof dish. Pour over orange juice and sprinkle with caster sugar. Place orange liqueur and brandy in a small saucepan and warm over a low heat, ignite, pour over crêpes and serve immediately.

ingredients

> ¹/2 cup/125 ml/4 fl oz orange juice, warmed
> **2 tablespoons caster sugar**
> **1 tablespoon orange-flavored liqueur**
> **1 tablespoon brandy**

crêpes

> **1 cup/125 g/4 oz flour**
> **³/4 cup/185 ml/6 fl oz milk**
> **¹/2 cup/125 ml/4 fl oz water**
> **2 eggs**
> **15 g/¹/2 oz butter, melted**
> **1 tablespoon sugar**

....
Serves 4

tip from the chef

To keep cooked crêpes warm while making the rest of the batch, place them in a stack on a heatproof plate and place in a low oven, or over a saucepan of simmering water. Alcohol needs to be warmed to flambé effectively, however, take care not to overheat or it will evaporate, before it you can ignite it.

cream
cheese cherry crêpes

■□□ I Cooking time: 15 minutes - Preparation time: 10 minutes

method

1. Combine cream cheese, kirsch, sugar and vanilla essence in a mixing bowl. Beat until smooth. Fold in cherries.
2. Spoon cheese mixture onto crêpes, fold in sides and roll up. Arrange crêpes in well greased ovenproof dish. Bake at 180°C/350°F/Gas 4 for 10 minutes.
3. Place reserved cherry liquid into a saucepan. Bring to the boil, reduce heat and whisk in cornflour mixture, stir until sauce thickens.
4. Arrange crêpes on serving plates, spoon over sauce and serve.

ingredients

> **240 g/8 oz cream cheese, softened**
> **2 tablespoons kirsch**
> **2 tablespoons superfine sugar**
> **1/2 teaspoon vanilla essence**
> **440 g/14 oz canned pitted black cherries, drained and liquid reserved**
> **6 crêpes**
> **2 teaspoons cornflour blended with 3 tablespoons water**

....
Serves 6

tip from the chef

Prepared crêpes are available in supermarkets and can be frozen so you have them on hand when needed.

yogurt
orange pancakes

■□□ | Cooking time: 20 minutes - Preparation time: 15 minutes

method

1. Sift together flour, salt and bicarbonate of soda into a mixing bowl. Make a well in the center. Combine yogurt, egg and milk and mix into flour mixture until just combined.

2. Drop spoonfuls of mixture into a lightly greased heavy-based frying pan and cook until bubbles form on the surface, then turn pancakes and cook on other side until golden.

3. To make sauce, place orange rind, juice and sugar in a saucepan and cook over a medium heat, stirring constantly, until sugar dissolves. Stir in cornflour mixture and cook for 1-2 minutes longer or until sauce thickens. Stir in Cointreau and heat for 1-2 minutes longer.

4. Top pancakes with sauce and accompany with extra yogurt.

....
Serves 4

ingredients

> 1 cup/125 g/4 oz flour
> 1/2 teaspoon salt
> 1/2 teaspoon bicarbonate of soda
> 1 1/4 cups/250 g/8 oz natural yogurt
> 1 egg, lightly beaten
> 1/3 cup/90 ml/3 fl oz milk
> natural yogurt, extra, to accompany

orange sauce

> 1 teaspoon finely grated orange rind
> 1/2 cup/125 ml/4 fl oz orange juice
> 2 tablespoons caster sugar
> 1 teaspoon cornflour blended with 2 teaspoons water
> 2 tablespoons Cointreau

tip from the chef

Pancakes, one of the quickest desserts you can make, can be prepared ahead of time then reheated prior to serving.

apple pudding
with ricotta cream

■□□ | Cooking time: 40 minutes - Preparation time: 10 minutes

ingredients

> 6 green apples, cored, peeled and cut into 1 cm/^{1}/$_2$ in slices
> 100 g/3^1/$_2$ oz raisins
> 60 g/2 oz pine nuts, toasted
> 1 cup/250 ml/8 fl oz orange juice
> ^{1}/$_4$ cup/90 g/3 oz honey
> ^{1}/$_2$ teaspoon ground cinnamon
> 6 whole cloves
> 1 tablespoon finely grated orange rind
> 60 g/2 oz ground almonds

ricotta cream

> 100 g/3^1/$_2$ oz ricotta cheese
> 100 g/3^1/$_2$ oz cottage cheese
> 1-2 tablespoons milk
> 1-2 tablespoons caster sugar

method

1. Layer apples, raisins and pine nuts in a shallow ovenproof dish. Pour over orange juice, drizzle with honey, then sprinkle with cinnamon, cloves, orange rind and almonds. Cover dish with aluminum foil and bake at 200°C/400°F/Gas 6 for 35-40 minutes or until apples are tender.
2. To make cream, place ricotta cheese and cottage cheese in a food processor or blender and process until smooth. Add a little milk if mixture is too thick and sweeten with sugar to taste.
3. Serve pudding hot or cold with a little ricotta cream.

....
Serves 4

tip from the chef

The ricotta cream served with this pudding is a delicious alternative to cream. You might like to try it as an accompaniment to other desserts.

wafer
stacks with pecan sauce

■ ■ □ | Cooking time: 25 minutes - Preparation time: 20 minutes

method

1. Beat egg white until soft peaks form. Gradually add sugar, beating well after each addition. Fold in vanilla essence, butter, hazelnuts and flour.

2. Place heaped teaspoons of mixture, 10 cm/4 in apart, on lightly greased baking trays. Spread mixture out to 5 cm/2 in diameter. Bake at 180°C/350°F/Gas 4 for 5 minutes or until edges are golden. Cool for 2-3 minutes before lifting on to wire racks to cool completely.

3. To make filling, place apples, honey and water in a saucepan. Bring to the boil, then cover and simmer 10-15 minutes or until apples are soft. Stir in sultanas and rind.

4. To make sauce, cook sugar and water until toffee is light golden. Remove from heat and carefully stir in cream. Stir over a medium heat until smooth. Stir in margarine and pecans.

5. Place one wafer on 4 plates, spread each with filling. Repeat with more wafers and filling to make a stack, finish with a wafer. Dust with icing sugar and spoon over sauce.

....

Serves 4

ingredients

> 1 egg white
> 3 tablespoons caster sugar
> 1/2 teaspoon vanilla essence
> 30 g/1 oz butter, melted
> 30 g/1 oz ground hazelnuts
> 3 tablespoons flour, sifted
> icing sugar to dust

apple filling

> 2 large green apples, cored, peeled and sliced thinly
> 2 tablespoons honey
> 4 tablespoons water
> 2 tablespoons sultanas
> 1 teaspoon grated lemon rind

pecan sauce

> 100 g/3 1/2 oz caster sugar
> 3 tablespoons water
> 125 ml/4 fl oz cream
> 45 g/1 1/2 oz margarine
> 3 tablespoons chopped pecans

tip from the chef

Granny Smith are the right apples to be used in this recipe.

chocolate
orange pumpkin pie

■□□ | Cooking time: 5 minutes - Preparation time: 15 minutes

ingredients

crumb crust
> 125 g/4 oz chocolate wafers, crushed
> 3 tablespoons finely chopped walnuts
> 6 tablespoons butter, melted

pumpkin filling
> 1 cup canned pumpkin
> 2 teaspoons grated orange rind
> 3/4 cup cream
> 2 eggs, separated
> 1 teaspoon apple pie spice
> 1/4 teaspoon ground nutmeg
> 2/3 cup brown sugar
> 1 1/2 tablespoons gelatin dissolved in 3 tablespoons hot water

method

1. To make crust, combine wafers and walnuts in a bowl. Stir in melted butter (a). Press mixture over base and sides of a 22.5 cm/ 9 in flan tin. Refrigerate.

2. To make filling, blend pumpkin, orange rind, 3 tablespoons cream, egg yolks, spice, nutmeg and sugar (b) until well mixed. Pour mixture into a saucepan and stir over medium heat until hot but not boiling. Whisk gelatin mixture into pumpkin mixture. Allow to cool, then refrigerate until almost set. Check every 15 minutes.

3. Whip remaining cream. Beat egg whites. Fold cream and egg whites into filling (c). Spoon into crust and refrigerate until set. Decorate top with cream and strawberries, if desired.

....
Serves 8

tip from the chef
Gelatin can be a little tricky if not used correctly. The dissolved gelatin and the food must be at similar temperatures before combining.

a

b

c

almond baskets

■■□ I Cooking time: 6 minutes - Preparation time: 20 minutes

method

1. Beat egg white with a fork until foamy. Gradually stir in icing sugar, vanilla essence, butter and almonds. Fold in flour (a).
2. Lightly grease baking trays. Mark 15 cm/6 in circles, using a saucer as a guide. Drop spoonfuls of mixture into circles; spread to fill circles (b). Bake at 220°C/425°F/Gas 7 for 5-6 minutes, or until cookies are light brown around edges.
3. Lift cookies quickly from trays. Carefully place cookies over upside-down small glasses or jars (c), to shape baskets around bottom. Hold until firm (this will take about 1 minute).
4. When cool, place a scoop of ice cream into each basket, pour caramel topping over, sprinkle with chopped almonds and serve.

ingredients

> **1 egg white**
> **4 tablespoons icing sugar, sifted**
> **1/2 teaspoon vanilla essence**
> **2 tablespoons butter, melted**
> **2 tablespoons ground almonds**
> **4 tablespoons flour, sifted**
> **vanilla ice cream**
> **caramel topping**
> **1/4 cup chopped almonds**

....
Serves 4

tip from the chef

Any filling such as fresh berries can be used with this delicious recipe. Fill and serve immediately to prevent biscuit softening.

a

b

c

apple
and berry plait

■ ■ □ | Cooking time: 45 minutes - Preparation time: 25 minutes

ingredients

> **24 sheets filo pastry**
> **1/2 cup melted butter**
> **icing sugar**

apple filling

> **360 g/12 oz canned apple pie filling**
> **1 teaspoon grated lemon rind**
> **3 tablespoons sultanas**
> **1 tablespoon honey**

berry filling

> **1 1/2 cups canned blueberries, drained**
> **3 tablespoons ground almonds**

method

1. Layer 8 filo pastry sheets on top of each other. Brush between each sheet with butter. Repeat with remaining pastry.
2. To make apple filling, combine apple, lemon rind, sultanas and honey. Spoon half the mixture down the long edge of one pastry layer, leaving 5 cm/2 in at each end, and roll up tightly. Repeat with remaining apple mixture and another pastry layer.
3. To make berry filling, combine blueberries and almonds. Spoon down remaining pastry layer as above.
4. Place rolls side by side on a baking tray, then form into a plait, tucking ends under. Brush with butter and bake at 190°C/375°F/Gas 5 for 40-45 minutes, until golden. Cool slightly and dust with icing sugar before serving.

....
Serves 4

tip from the chef
When working with filo pastry, cover any sheets that are not immediately in use with a dampened tea-towel to prevent drying.

italian roll

■ ■ □ | Cooking time: 15 minutes - Preparation time: 20 minutes

method

1. Place eggs in a large mixing bowl and beat until thick and creamy. Add sugar a little at a time, beating well after each addition until sugar dissolves and mixture thickens. Fold in flour alternately with milk.

2. Spoon mixture into a lightly greased and lined 25 x 30 cm/10 x 12 in baking tray. Bake at 180°C/350°F/Gas 4 for 12-15 minutes or until firm. Turn out onto a sheet of greaseproof paper, remove lining paper and trim edges. Roll up from the narrow end, using paper to lift and guide roll. Stand for 5 minutes, then unroll and allow to cool.

3. To make filling, place ricotta cheese, icing sugar, vanilla essence and crème de cacao in a mixing bowl and beat until well combined. Fold in chocolate and glacé fruit and spread over cake. Re-roll and transfer to a serving platter. Spread with cream and decorate with grated chocolate.

ingredients

> 3 eggs
> 125 g/4 oz caster sugar
> 90 g/3 oz self-raising flour, sifted
> 2 tablespoons hot milk
> 125 g/4 fl oz cream, whipped
> 60 g/2 oz chocolate, grated

ricotta filling

> 250 g/8 oz ricotta cheese
> 4 tablespoons icing sugar
> 1/2 teaspoon vanilla essence
> 1 tablespoon crème de cacao
> 30 g/1 oz chocolate, grated
> 1 tablespoon chopped glacé fruit

....
Serves 8

tip from the chef

For a different stuffing, use ground cinnamon instead of liqueur and nuts of your choice instead of glacé fruit.

double
choc log

■ ■ □ | Cooking time: 20 minutes - Preparation time: 20 minutes

method

1. Place egg yolks and sugar in a bowl and beat until thick and pale. Stir in chocolate, flour and cocoa powder.
2. Place egg whites in a clean bowl and beat until stiff peaks form. Fold egg whites into chocolate mixture.
3. Pour mixture into a greased and lined 26 x 32 cm/10^1/$_2$ x 12^3/$_4$ in baking tray and bake at 180°C/350°F/Gas 4 for 15 minutes or until firm. Turn cake onto a tea-towel sprinkled with caster sugar and roll up from short end. Remove paper. Set aside to cool.
4. To make filling, place white chocolate in a heatproof bowl over a saucepan of simmering water and heat, stirring, until smooth. Add cream and stir until combined. Cover and chill until thickened and of a spreadable consistency. Unroll cake and spread with filling leaving a 1 cm/^{1}/$_2$ in border. Re-roll cake.
5. To make icing, mix chocolate and butter until combined. Spread icing over roll and then, using a spatula, roughly texture the icing. Refrigerate.

ingredients

> 5 eggs, separated
> ^{1}/$_4$ cup/60 g/2 oz caster sugar
> 100 g/3^1/$_2$ oz dark chocolate, melted and cooled
> 2 tablespoons self-raising flour, sifted
> 2 tablespoons cocoa powder, sifted

white chocolate filling

> 60 g/2 oz white chocolate
> ^{2}/$_3$ cup/170 ml/5^1/$_2$ fl oz double cream

chocolate icing

> 200 g/6^1/$_2$ oz dark chocolate, melted
> 60 g/2 oz butter, melted

....
Serves 8

tip from the chef

Keep this dessert refrigerated until served. Dust log with icing sugar to create "snow" just before serving.

chestnut log

■ ■ □ | Cooking time: 5 minutes - Preparation time: 20 minutes

method

1. Combine chestnut purée, butter, egg, vanilla essence and half the rum in a bowl until smooth. Grease and line the bottom and sides of a 20 x 12.5 cm/8 x 5 in loaf tin with biscuits and sprinkle with remaining rum. Spoon in chestnut mixture; top with biscuits. Refrigerate until firm, turn log out onto a serving platter.

2. To make glaze, combine cocoa powder, sugar and water in a heatproof bowl over a saucepan of simmering water. Stir until sugar has dissolved and glaze is smooth. Cool and brush three-quarters of the glaze over log.

3. To make icing, cream together icing sugar, butter and coffee. Beat until well blended. Decorate log with piped rosettes of icing and drizzle over remaining glaze. Serve sliced with ice cream, if desired.

ingredients

> **440 g/14 oz canned sweetened chestnut purée**
> **1/2 cup butter, softened**
> **1 egg**
> **2-3 drops vanilla essence**
> **4 tablespoons rum**
> **24 sponge biscuits**

glaze

> **2 tablespoons cocoa powder**
> **1 tablespoon superfine sugar**
> **2 tablespoons water**

icing

> **3/4 cup icing sugar**
> **1/2 cup butter, softened**
> **1 tablespoon very strong coffee, cooled**

....
Serves 8

tip from the chef
*If brewed coffee is unavailable, substitute
1 teaspoon of instant coffee dissolved
in 1 tablespoon hot water.*

strawberry
cheesecake

■□□ | Cooking time: 50 minutes - Preparation time: 15 minutes

ingredients

> 1/2 cup plain flour
> 1/2 cup wholemeal self-raising flour
> 60 g/2 oz butter
> 1 egg yolk
> 1-2 tablespoons apple juice

ricotta filling

> 250 g/1/2 lb ricotta cheese
> 1/2 cup yogurt
> 2 eggs
> 2 tablespoons lemon juice
> 1/4 cup sugar

strawberry topping

> 250 g/1/2 lb strawberries
> 3/4 cup thickened cream, whipped

method

1. Sift flours into a bowl, rub in butter. Add egg yolk and enough apple juice to mix to a soft dough. Knead on lightly floured surface until smooth. Press evenly over base of a 23 cm/9 in springform tin. Cover with a sheet of greaseproof paper, cover paper with uncooked rice or beans. Bake in moderately hot oven for 8 minutes. Remove paper and rice, bake for a further 8 minutes or until golden brown. Cool.

2. To make filling, beat ricotta cheese, yogurt, eggs, lemon juice and sugar in a small bowl with an electric mixer until smooth. Pour over pastry base, bake in moderate oven for 30 minutes or until set, cool.

3. To make topping, purée half the strawberries, strain to remove seeds. Spread over top of cheesecake, decorate with remaining strawberries and whipped cream.

Serves 8

tip from the chef

Preheat oven and control temperature during cooking. If it is too high the cheesecake may get burnt in the outside and remain uncooked inside.

cassata siciliana

■□□ | Cooking time: 0 minute - Preparation time: 15 minutes

method

1. Beat ricotta cheese and sugar together until light and fluffy. Divide mixture in half. Fold pistachios and fruit into half of mixture. Mix cinnamon, chocolate and amaretto into other half. Cover and set aside.

2. Line base and sides of a 20 cm/8 in mold with plastic food wrap, then with one of cake slices. Fill with fruit mixture and top with remaining cake slice. Cover and freeze for 2 hours or overnight. Pour chocolate mixture over, freeze until set.

3. To make topping, whip cream and amaretto together until soft peaks form. Just prior to serving, turn out cassata, spread completely with cream and decorate with glacé fruit.

Serves 8

ingredients

> 500 g/1 lb ricotta cheese
> 250 g/8 oz sugar
> 2 tablespoons chopped pistachios
> 3 tablespoons chopped glacé fruit
> 1/4 teaspoon ground cinnamon
> 60 g/2 oz dark chocolate, grated
> 2 tablespoons amaretto liqueur
> 2 slices sponge cake, 20 cm/8 in diameter and 1 cm/1/2 in thick each

topping

> 250 ml/8 fl oz cream
> 1 tablespoon amaretto liqueur
> selection of glacé fruit

tip from the chef

A simple do-ahead dinner party dessert that looks spectacular when decorated with extra glacé fruit. It is best prepared a day before serving.

strawberry
shortbread fan

■ ■ ☐ | Cooking time: 45 minutes - Preparation time: 25 minutes

method

1. To make shortbread, combine flour, icing sugar and ground rice in a large mixing bowl. Rub in butter, using fingertips, until mixture resembles coarse breadcrumbs. Stir in lemon rind and vanilla essence. Turn onto a floured surface and knead until smooth. Roll out to 5 mm/1/4 in thick and, using a 20 cm/8 in cake tin as a guide, cut out a circle. Place on a greased and lined baking tray.

2. Mark 12 wedges on shortbread and bake at 160°C/325°F/Gas 3 for 40 minutes or until lightly browned. Cut into wedges and cool on tray. Spread one side of each wedge with chocolate and set aside until chocolate sets.

3. To make crème pâtissiere, place egg, egg yolks, flour, cornflour, sugar and vanilla essence in a small bowl and whisk to combine. Stir 2 tablespoons of hot milk into egg mixture, then stir mixture into remaining milk and cook over a low heat, stirring constantly, until mixture thickens. Cool. Fold in whipped cream.

4. To assemble, spread sponge with crème pâtissiere and arrange shortbread wedges, angled upwards, on sponge with halved strawberries tucked between each wedge.

Serves 12

ingredients

> 12 strawberries, halved
> 1 x 20 cm/8 in round sponge cake

shortbread

> 1 cup/125 g/4 oz flour, sifted
> 30 g/1 oz icing sugar, sifted
> 30 g/1 oz ground rice, sifted
> 125 g/4 oz butter, cubed
> 1/2 teaspoon finely grated lemon rind
> 1/2 teaspoon vanilla essence
> 100 g/31/2 oz dark chocolate, melted

crème pâtissiere

> 1 egg
> 2 egg yolks
> 4 teaspoons flour, sifted
> 4 teaspoons cornflour, sifted
> 1/4 cup/60 g/2 oz caster sugar
> 1 teaspoon vanilla essence
> 11/4 cups/310 ml/ 10 fl oz milk, scalded
> 1/2 cup/125 ml/4 fl oz double cream, whipped

tip from the chef

Accompany with strawberry coulis, if desired.

index